LETDOWN

Sonia Greenfield

Sonia

WHITE PINE PRESS / BUFFALO, NEW YORK

White Pine Press
P.O. Box 236
Buffalo, NY 14201
www.whitepine.org

Publication of this book was made possible by funds from the National Endowment for the Arts, which believes that a great nation deserves great art; by public funds from the New York State Council on the Arts, with the support of Governor Andrew M. Cuomo and the New York State Legislature, a State Agency; and with the support of Robert Alexander.

Grateful acknowledgment is made to the editors of the following publications where versions of these individual pieces first appeared:

Nos. 4, 23, and 29 appeared in *Cultural Weekly.* Nos. 18 and 22 appeared in *Verse-Virtual.* Nos. 17 and 26 appeared in *Salamander.* No. 41 appeared in *Yes, Poetry.* No. 45 appeared in *Ragazine.* No. 49 appeared in *sidereal magazine.* Nos. 51, 52, and 58 appeared in *Mom Egg* and *Mom Egg VOX.* No. 59 appeared in *Rattle's Poets Respond.* No. 60 appeared in *Lullaby of Teeth: An Anthology of Southern California Poetry,* Moon Tide Press, 2017. No. 67 appeared in *Poet Lore.*

Cover design by Jennika Smith.

Printed and bound in the United States of America.

ISBN 978-1-945680-35-9

Library of Congress number: 2019944715

Acknowledgments

Big hugs to the following people who helped me parse this difficult material: Jessica Johnson, Megan Snyder-Camp, Sara Wainscott, Meredith Lewis, Allison Harter, Charles Brown, Jinny Koh, David Ulin, Dinah Lenney, Sherine Gilmour, Martin Ott, Max Heinegg, and Christina Wolfgram.

Many thanks to Amy Gerstler and Claudia Rankine—it was in your workshops where these prose poems first took shape.

A final note of appreciation for Nickole Brown and Robert Alexander: Thank you for believing in this project. May it find the readership that needs it.

For my son—

"If you run away," said his mother,
"I will run after you. For you are my little bunny."

—Margaret Wise Brown

Letdown

The kissed child puts his hand at last back into his mother's,
though it is not the same;
her fine face neither right nor wrong, only thoroughly his.

—Jane Hirshfield

Foreword

They used to believe the *mis-* of miscarriage was payment for a mis-deed. But there are two shadow halves here. Two threads to the story. One, failure. The other, diagnosis.

I ask another member of my default sisterhood if she questions whether some *mis-* of the body set her son askew on earth, because we always find ourselves blaming our eggs, our age, our appetites.

From Connecticut to Washington to California, every place I fled to, all the mothers I've met have assumed responsibility. We've read the latest studies. We tally our mixed blessings.

I didn't drink; then I edit memory and imagine I did. What did I put in my body or what was put in my body? Otherwise, why?

All my life I never knew what to say or how to be, so I wonder whether disorder was born in me.

Letdown

1.

I checked Kent town records for the defunct New England graveyard by the farm, its effaced stones facing away from the road, a plot where burials were common and children were begat as oxen to plant then plow the fields.

I find the Engels' fourteen children minus nine taken by diphtheria, eater of children. I look it up: the skin took on a bluish tone and a black, fibrous cover was a plug in the throat: mothers made to watch what running out of air looks like, to offer names, then plant the dirt with them.

My gait swung heavy as I picked my way among stones crackling with morning frost in the hollow's wintering cemetery, the smallest markers toppled flat like pavers. I worked my way around instead, keeping a safe distance, refusing to cross that history.

2.

At fifteen-and-a-half weeks, I experienced a quickening like popcorn popping or a faint finger drumming on a small table. Somewhere around eighteen weeks, a plucked nylon guitar string, the music acoustic, not electric, fingers rolling off strings like lazy strumming. The inside of my belly, the body of a guitar. In the early twenties, you kicked your father in the ear, and he was endeared. At twenty-eight, a dryer drum tumbled balled-up socks. At thirty weeks, an earthquake. Hard spots and soft spots, a whole, small body moving in there. All the way around, from below my breasts to just above my pubic bone. You slept when I slept and stayed with me through winter.

3.

After the snow, mud season. I mucked about, duck-booted, with your little feet rolling like ballpoints, writing from your Jonah's prison on the round red wall, your small cell in salt and sea. What did you say? You tallied another day with toe taps against my carillon of ribs as you rocked in my muscle sling to tunes on the radio. The crocus sprouts shot through spring goo, which meant time almost served, sweet convict, at thirty-eight weeks already perfectly pitched and articulate.

4.

I want to describe it, to tell the whole story, but the birthing suite and its muted walls were details lost in rage. And the Joni Mitchell I played—the candy of her voice—could not be heard over my retching. That all the ways I thought I had prepared were like closing a sliding door on a tsunami. That I couldn't listen to myself whimper anymore, the anesthesiologist floating to me like a goddess in institutional blue while I leaned over, trembling, as the thick, blissful needle slipped deep into my back while I hugged the ball of you.

How this is the point where *what was* should overlay on top of *what should have been.* That your heart decelerated, machines binged, and your father fetched the nurse. That nurses and doctor rocked my dead legs back and forth to dislodge you. That I had to push you out before full dilation, my cervix tearing. And the doctor was stitching for so long. And you, glistening violet, looked me in the face. And the minute you latched on, I became remade in your image. That I would have liked to do it again. But by the time it was possible, I couldn't.

5.

I can't help but make symbols of them. In the Hall of Birds, for example, we walk the glass walls of wings pinned in static flight, a vole dripping from the mouth of the barn owl, but I'm looking at the common kind for reference. In the backyard, it must have been a nuthatch nest laid to waste the morning I woke to what sounded like a crying dog. It was a blue jay marauding with a shriek, and she left with claws full when all week prior another sat in that camellia's crown, tending what hatched.

Or at our cabin, where I carried you through those late winter months, tracking the mating pair of geese. In the dark, after the hatching, they honked their horns of distress while I birthed a boy in sterile light, at three in the morning, in the wing of a hospital. Then the smell of my own blood lingered for weeks as I counted down the goslings to zero. Back at our cabin in the woods, you bawling as the sun tiptoed into the hollow. It must have been a red-breasted sapsucker that played the metal gutters every dawn, hammering my fatigue home until I begged your father to kill it. The bird's machine-gun report answered by shotgun. That resonance still traveling as the crow flies.

6.

Postpartum, you were an island because you could not yet roll, and I was your castaway. The waters were lush with kelp where dark shapes refusing to take shape swam close. The television was blue, the living room became Shark Week, and commercials suggested medicines I might take for my symptoms, multifarious like shark teeth because when one tooth falls out, another grows to replace it. A surfer's curved scar proved that one can live with a chunk missing. We could not stay marooned forever.

When sleep finally came, I dreamt of insomnia and wandered the house as a clothesline squeaked a yard over. Awake, you were up and down like my moods. I sat at the edge of the bed and my ears pivoted. I could see in the dark. I checked your small chest again for its rise and fall. I checked with a pocket mirror for your moist breath.

7.

Winter snapshot: the sky is orange and gold and cold, stranger than heat from a blue flame. I hear the whistle blow on the teakettle, watch the steam dissipate. Your father shuffles off the dead to care for the living, blood soaking the blue leg of his scrubs. Another night in the hospital stripped away and shoved in the wash. The moon, earth, and sun arc around like Christmas toys that tick off the years. The winter builds ice floes that melt and freeze. The camera sets time still with a flash, or so I wish. Your baby clothes are folded into postage stamps, put in boxes, and mailed to the garage, the basement, the empty room inside me.

8.

Late summer, the sun was supple as I rolled your stroller to the canal where boats left a wake of mirrors as they rounded the bend. You watched and listened, or at least your eyes were dazzled by ripples lapping toward you.

It's just as I used to do with my grandfather when we rolled down to the river in his '76 Caddy. It was our way to see time pass. Now my grandfather is long gone. The lookout point gone, and if not gone, then lost to what I have left behind.

Yet here we are, generations keeping our clock by passing boats desperate for one last run before the weather takes a turn. This is how we make memory indelible: first, sailboat; then, speedboat; then, little skiff.

9.

The Weather Channel runs the local forecast on the eights, and we miss it, so we try again as the laundry is laundered, the dishwasher washes, and you toddle like a toddler.

Clouds close and part. Tulips litter red petals. A gutter sluice sounds like applause.

The neighbors bring you galoshes and say there is no bad weather only bad clothes, but we hold out like lonely daters with high standards. It's just another day waiting for paradise to unfold for us, a day where drops from a broken gutter keep time on the porch while everything else tries to take it.

10.

Frank O'Hara, my sentimental doppelgänger, can write birthday poems to Rachmaninoff whom he never knew but loved, and I cradle my little boy blue—today you're two—*by the blue windows in the blue light of rain* because I can't write lines that matter, I'm so dumb with love. Is it because I need distance to set music to what is weighty, just like the tears that fall from my eyes right into yours?

11.

Anaphylaxis: the kebab eaters dripped yogurt sauce on their pants and tipped their heads back with a laugh, their teeth flashing in the rare Seattle sunlight, which also glinted on sea glass and china embedded in the patio, and the gelato shop scooped its scoops while the statue of Lenin judged how we were capitalizing on a good neighborhood spot to people-watch, Lebanese music a lantern of warmth.

Everything was drenched with gold, so we were surprised when your face swelled shut. No paperclip in an outlet, no vicious dog on the loose: just sesame flavoring falafel we shared with your toddler mouth, and suddenly death lurked wearing all white, was a waxen tear drop, a little seed that can fit on the head of a pin.

Your eyelids smothered your eyes, and your lips were blisters: tahini's one-two punch.

12.

The down on your back whorls to the center like a fingerprint. My hands follow the direction of your spiral, slicking it down with lotion. In baby photos you are mottled with eczema, but you are smooth, something like a boy now. Your fuzz darkening, the finest mustache shadowing your lip. Your lashes, blue-black fringes. Here is the pleasure of ritual: my hands up and down your limbs until your skin sings—what we can heal with a little touch and love and grease. At storytime, you weave a stuffed-animal's tassel between your fingers while sucking your thumb, and I read to you about small fish fighting back or Harold's purple crayon drawing the world right where he needs it.

13.

As we crawled through the interchange, late sunlight glaring off game-day traffic, you seized. I stopped hard, mid-lane, and punched the hazards as you bucked against your car seat.

I wouldn't say I *watched*, couldn't say I *stared*, won't say I *saw* when your mouth went slack and your eyes rolled white. All I could do was *throb*.

The ambulance met me where I stopped between three major freeways. Later, your fever lingered, and your brown eyes brimmed like a calf's. You clung to me while I sat and let my own sweat rise.

What could I do otherwise?

14.

I try to teach you how to blow dandelion parachutes as we pluck the stalks, but you rub the grey heads on the pavement and the seeds skitter along the sidewalk.

Some days I feel my bloom fading. I'm a little like a weed gone to seed—I see how you grow toward the sun and take root in the compost of my slow decay. Most days my seeds land on nothing but concrete.

15.

We walk the reservoir after dark where a neighbor has festooned palm fronds with ornaments and a strand of white lights spiraling the length of the trunk. It's all Christmas facsimile, another neighbor's colored bulbs blink the night still as if real snow lent us its muffled quiet.

We pull icicles from newspaper and hang them on a tree; we pull angels from a tree and wrap them in the same old news.

Years ago, my grandfather pointed to the sky and said he heard sleigh bells. Now, you race to a house animated by bells ringing with silence. You see a clamor of color pushing off the night, which is magic we both believe in.

16.

The second time I scooped the full heat of your body, I felt as if you could set your preschool on fire.

I gave you Tylenol and pulled you into bed, your temperature wavering around 102. I sucked my teeth and placed my hand on your head until we both slept. You woke me by flopping around like a fish drowning in air. I called for your father who said, *Give him room, let him finish,* then I said, *Oh God, Oh God, Oh God.* Your father said your temperature was 104.3.

Afterwards, you could only drool, and your eyes rolled around as flat and blank as unstamped pennies, the postictal state going on and on until one-by-one your generators flared back to life. *Postictal* meaning reboot, meaning liminal state. The Tylenol didn't work when I was told it would. I'm sorry.

17.

All I could think about were cells dividing. Clean separations. The body's regular rebirth.

Each of the hospital ward's doors were closed. Each door, a sign. Each sign, a character. Your name written above the furl of Batman's black cape. Behind doors, cells split, though not with grace. All the doors had a second, plain sign that said *Stay Away* and *Wash Your Hands*, and I muttered *of this place.*

Even the fountain in the courtyard knew uniformity is a farce, so its small water flowers, six in all, bloomed from the pool in different sizes. You pointed this out because all I saw were windows streaked with the dirty remnants of rain long since spent. Most fountains have been drained since the drought, but this one keeps up with the work of diversion, trying to make us see past what must look bad.

18.

We search the spring for carnivals and find St. Charles in Toluca Lake, so we go, as if we could drive by all those neon rides etching their geometry onto the sky. Dirt on our feet, a shattered rainbow of raffle tickets confetti the ground, and kiddie cars turn you in tight circles twice, punctuating your dusk with delight.

It could be thirty years ago: teens in crop tops, goldfish in plastic bags, ribbed beer cups in the hands of red-faced men who clearly need a drink. A hotel band does its best with oldies as grannies toe tap to "All Shook Up."

Missing are hot zeppoles in greasy bags and the Virgin Mary pinned with dollars. Otherwise, I could be you, again: wind pressing your eyes closed, mosquito bites big as quarters, the flying swings spinning your heart out on a chain, as fireworks become exclamation points sparking the sky with chromatic rain.

19.

Another heat wave, and succulents send up pink kerchiefs. The grass dries, a match width's distance from fire. We make our way to the field below the sign where dogs chase balls and tourists pretend to hold up HOLLYWOOD for pictures. A hawk finds an updraft, lives in the moment, and you do your best on the jungle gym. Your bangs curl with sweat.

On the way back, the road hugs many-chambered homes and sometimes a grand piano makes music, or sometimes it just sits in the wide window and bleaches in the Los Angeles sun. Once we get inside, we're all the same—many-chambered, dependent on grace. On the electric box at the bottom of the hill, I find street art of a man with a bird's head, and it has a written reminder for me: *You already have everything you need.*

20.

Multiple Punctate Bilateral White Matter Lesions. It was a slow Thursday on the ER's swing shift. The usual except for a boy's brain printed on pieces of paper: MRI pictures of lateral sections. A nurse walked the white hall down to radiology for the read. Images showed the structural underpinnings of a face known for three beauty marks, also a skull slightly flattened on one side from a long road trip east to west at three months old. The nurse is your father.

These could represent areas of focal gliosis, the radiologist wrote. Translation: a hot poker left pointillations on your front subcortical white matter. *Alternatively, these could also represent areas of demyelination such as acute encephalomyelitis.* Translation: when you put your dirty thumb in your mouth, some virus climbed in. *Another possibility would be for a primary demyelinating process.* Translation: genetically fucked. Your brain eating itself. *There is a mucosal thickening of the paranasal sinuses.* Translation: you had a head cold. I had to grab a tissue before you wiped your nose with your hand.

We had to wait a week for diagnosis.

21.

I take you to a friend's house to see what she knows. What can I learn from her taupe couches and worn philosophy books lining the shelves? What can I divine from the dirty snow piling up on the sides of the cul-de-sac?

You drag your leg cast across the living room and reach for cookies nutty with allergens. Her husband moves like a cat and fills the love seat. She is a cancer survivor, her face still holding the summer sun, wrinkles assembling into a smile cracked open by you.

We discuss *their* boy and her husband lets out a little grief. It hangs in the air between us as complex as a snowflake. I don't ask. I know they had a son whose bar mitzvah I went to twenty years ago when streamers and Looney Tunes could ward off darkness.

I found out later the son went into the woods where college grounds gave way to a precipice slickened with loam, and he never made it back.

22.

Joy is pocket-sized. Like quarter rides. We could ignore the patina of grime on the pagodas in Chinatown where dusk dropped wet against the steamed window of the dumpling shop, which was one bead on a string that went herb shop, gold Buddha shop, bonsai shop, repeat, until pinwheels in the pinwheel store turned to the breeze and you said, *Bye, wind,* then blew kisses I tried to catch.

I carried pockets so full of quarters we jingled as we headed past the koi fountain teeming with ghost fish, past the old smoking man, past lanterns sunburned red to pink to the plaza where paint-flecked rides bucked against the gloom, and we paid again and again until the mechanical frog churned and galloped you all the way past believing we would ever find ourselves empty-handed.

23.

EEG Creation Date: 15:29:39, Aug. 23, 2012. I think the brain is rivers of electricity, is cities of electricity, that it looks like a metropolis from an airplane. Your electricity is learning new routes, like how to work around *gliosis.* Little scars. Little scares. Your EEG is a paper of squiggly lines, a code, each line telling the story of impulses, some lines quivering with uncertainty. In the office I said, *Look, now you get to become a robot,* as the tech gelled wires to your head. I said, *Look, you are a handsome sheik who must be still,* with a white sheet wrapped around multicolored wires plugged into a silver box with a heavy cord leading to a computer that wrote thirty-one lines about your brain. I said, *Look, the computer just wrote a poem about your legs and how they have a mind of their own.* I said, *Let's beep like robots.* I said, *Don't move now.* I said, *Okay, tell me how old you are again.* You said, *Free.* That's right. Free.

24.

Focal: that sweet unguent glue of hose water and sweat plastered your hair like a frame for your face, and the ball careened across the yard as the dog tried to get her teeth around it, and we yelled, *Emmy, no!* as we ran in wider circles, and the sun let up a little bit as the clock's small hand swung westward, and the ball kept getting kicked under summer's emerald vines as you practiced screaming loudest, and then some unseen scissors came and snipped your marionette strings so one second you were trilling and the next your head connected with a sick thunk against the wet driveway.

25.

Focal, local, multiple occurrences: running through the house with that energy spike just before bed and you're taking a sharp curve around the dining table past the rattling china, you skim the brown carpet, and you're practically a hovercraft as the dogs chase or get chased until you fall forward and shriek, *Help!* as your legs become electrified with spasms, your top half crawling along, your bottom half in a freakish jig. Postictal: your legs unresponsive. We didn't know whether they would run again.

26.

A baby was rolled into your room. His crib was capped with a plastic lid like an old-fashioned animal pen. We listened as he never cried, instead offering up his babble to the clinical half-darkness, alone, his story unspeakable. Then the scent of glue used to attach nodes to your skull smelled like huffing. That, plus the bundle of wires attached were every color, like art in the wrong place.

A boy who shared your room had ten grand mals heard from our side of the veil, my nerves rattled by the chomp and clatter of his jaw. We could see how his own brain did him in, that he *just wasn't right* we might say as they have said to us. Of you. Sad to see the effects of what hard science can't control, to know only a sliding curtain hemisphered him from you.

Meanwhile, doctors rounded in roving packs offering the word *discharge*. To think when you sleep electrical impulses *discharge* and arc wrong, something just short of seizure belied by your face in repose, black lashes like a ruffle of ferns.

The seat where I spent the night reminded me that sometimes sleep comes to get us through. . . . No, merely to carry us into an uncertain morning when medical machines wake us with alarms.

27.

Your Psychological Evaluation. *A four-year-old Caucasian boy who was referred with concerns regarding autism spectrum disorder: 1. Deficits in social-emotional reciprocity. YES. 2. Deficits in nonverbal communicative behaviors used for social interactions. YES. 3. Deficits in developing, maintaining, and understanding relationships. YES. 4. Stereotyped or repetitive motor movements, use of objects, or speech. YES. 5. Insistence on sameness, inflexible adherence to routines, or ritualized patterns of verbal or nonverbal behaviors. YES. 6. Highly restricted, fixated interests that are abnormal in intensity or focus. MAYBE.*

In summary, using the DSM-V—meets the criteria for an Autism Spectrum Disorder. He shows persistent deficits in social communication and social interaction across multiple contexts and has repetitive patterns of behavior, interests, and activities. His symptoms have been present since early development and they cause significant impairment in important areas of social and academic functioning.

28.

Some days you serve word salad and long moments of silence. You say, *Mama, I like doing everything,* as if that means anything to anyone but you. You make eye contact, and contrary to textbook lore, you grab me around the neck and pull me to you. You leave lingering kisses on the mouth of a babysitter. You can't decide if Rufus Wainwright's voice is worth crying for, so you cry because you can't decide.

The world overwhelms you with its clang and glare. So what if you've pushed a baby or two? When I was in kindergarten, I pulled a chair out from under a boy who was sitting down. I was surprised when he cried. Is it wrong when we drive and let our silence pull us forward as if the cab of our car is a music box? Our car is like a needle in the road's groove, and we hum.

29.

They found the body of the nonverbal boy in the East River. He was obsessed with subways. It is said they all love trains.

Twice today we rode the rails on a miniature train going nowhere through tunnels, everything scaled down so we straddle the passenger car of a steamer smaller than a Fiat. We chuff near a three-tree grove of pomelos, past a water wheel lifting toy troughs to the sky, through a ghost town—stained-glass church and courthouse haunted by skeletons the size of your hand.

Back again by delicate red-haired boys shunting something like love with their scrappy Santa Fe engines. Too old for this, they tinker and avoid eye contact as if I might glimpse the future there. All around toddlers in engineer overalls swarm like ants to sugar, winter's sun gilding cowlicks copper and gold.

30.

The small print on your pill bottle: *Side Effects: You Should Know That Your Mental Health May Change in Unexpected Ways and You May Become Suicidal (Thinking about Harming or Killing Yourself or Planning or Trying to Do So) While You Are Taking Oxcarbazepine.*

What could you possibly understand about not being here?

As much as the deer who ran from snapping twigs as we crossed New England's wet March in my third trimester with you or as much as a boy who won't jump from the monkey bars no matter how much I coax.

You have crying jags when you can't spread your towel on the grass or when your shoe won't clasp. I was going to say that I can't imagine you not here either, but I have had to wonder what I would do with your things if I were without you.

It's okay. I have crying jags, too.

31.

We were waiting in line for another train in Griffith Park, you a-twitch and too busy with your hands. A woman was there with her granddaughter. She told me how she no longer judges people on first sight, and she told me how people thought her two-year-old grandson was "a bad seed." That it was medications making him bloated and ill-tempered. Her granddaughter— silent as an old film star—wore small gold hoops. An only child now, she touched my hand with gravitas. The bad seed was leukemia. Then the bell clanged, the conductor said, *All aboard!* and time snapped forward.

32.

Your father wanted me to say *we* made the decision to have no more children. Now everything feels fraught: the young mother dragging two boys in her trampy grip down Sunset Boulevard; my teenage abortions as simple subtraction, as if babies were just arithmetic; the single tiny sock, a symbol, a scrap of red waving from the chain-link fence; my boxes of motherhood, the detritus of longing, cluttering the garage; my little boy rolling his wooden train down the track, the *loneliest number* crooning from the stereo.

33.

Side Effects: we're titrating up one medication, so we must watch for your skin's necrosis. And we're titrating down one medication, so we must watch for your urge to be no more: suicide by child. Another medication controls repetition, keeps impulses in check. Of it, we must watch for stomach ulcers. Side effects of diagnoses of an only child include new neuroses, requiring I watch you sleep, somehow hearing my own heart beating in the measured rise and fall of your chest.

34.

We're at the zoo where the Los Angeles sun makes the animals wilt. *These are Cayugas*, the volunteer tells us. The drake's sheen is an oil slick, like Elvis, iridescent, opalescent like a fig beetle, so you don't even see the hen tending to her hatchlings. She's dull, sometimes dun or flat black with a few white feathers. Like me as I shed plumage to raise you, who finds me bright and downy anyway, at the zoo where we watch ducks swagger and strut.

35.

Side Effects: Ever since your wings sprouted, I keep trying to tether you, but you flutter off before I can reach your ankle. Your feathers mostly lie flat and fold between your bony shoulder blades like a little backpack no one sees but me. Alone, you spread them wide for me, their gloss like rivulets of water, the sound of their opening like a breeze rattling the dry palms lining our streets, fronds still clinging to the trees.

36.

You continue to try and understand words. I say, *eventually,* and you ask what it means. I say, *Something won't happen now, but it will happen soon.* I try to explain how some words have two or more meanings. For example, *letdown.*

When you were born, you latched on to fill the bowl of your hunger. You pulled and pulled, then I pumped three ounces of pure colostrum into a bottle the size of your father's thumb, and you drained that. Then my milk came in with a rush. We were synchronized. Once, when you were eight months old, I rode something like a centrifuge at the fall carnival, and when I stepped off the ride, two wet circles on my shirt marked me as your mother.

Also, per the dictionary: let·down [let-doun] *noun* I. a decrease in volume, force, energy, etc.: *a letdown in egg production.* 2. disillusionment, discouragement, or disappointment: *Her husband's earlier refusal for more children was a letdown.* 3. depression; deflation: *She felt a terrible letdown at the end of her fertility.*

37.

Someone says to me, *This is really about shame, isn't it?* Shame in that I can't be satisfied with what I have. Someone says to me, *Well, we're all a little bit on the spectrum, right?* And this comes from a place of kindness. Someone says to me, *You chose to put your professional life before seeking motherhood.* But that wasn't it. I waited until I was safe. Someone says to me, *You never know what's going to happen.* So be afraid, be elated. Someone says to me, *We really appreciate what makes your son unique.* (Subtext: But there's still something wrong with him.) Someone says to me, *He seems normal to me.* Someone says to me, *We always thought he seemed a little off.* Off what? Someone says to me, *This is all just because you wanted another baby.* I knew I was to blame. Someone says to me, *Why can't you be happy with what you have?* Someone says to me, *It's all in God's hands. It's part of his plan.* Tell your God to play nice. Someone says to me, *Don't be so in love with your own suffering.* I just wanted a little more. Why is that so wrong?

38.

According to the newsletter I signed up for, I was only in the fifth week, the heartbeat to come a week or two later.

I had a dream, and in it, I could see the shape of a hand through the skin of my belly. I was awakened by a tingling in my breasts, which also registered as dream. And just as I knew before I really knew, I also knew I wasn't anymore the minute I saw the first drop of blood. I checked in, and the body said, *Sorry, no.*

Then you said, *You're okay,* and patted my head. The dogs crowded around my face to lick the salt off. Your father didn't know how to turn both to me and away. Accidents happen, they say. Even to my last chance.

With your father I said, *Please,* and he said, *No.* I said, *Please,* and he said, *No.* I said, *Please,* and he said, *Yes.* He said, *Yes,* but my body could not answer in kind.

39.

After the procedure, they give young women juice and cookies. Time to recover. There were two instances, but they overlay as identical. Let's say that it was fall the first time and summer the next.

I didn't have a car and the bus ride was long. My chart had two circle stickers on the tab for two visits. The ride there was, first time, sun at a cooling angle, the colors of the phoenix, and then, second time, sun right above, hot, the phoenix risen. I sank away into gassed darkness, then the ride back was contractions for ninety minutes on a public bus, was end-of-day, end-of-day.

When it's bad, I say my payment has been you—perfect, flawed you—and the bright cabochon of blood dazzling red on the toilet paper in the light from the bathroom window a week after testing positive with what should have been your sister or brother—five conceptions, two abortions, one live birth.

Forgive me, but on very bad days I have to push away this feeling: that I was cheated out of a second chance to get it right.

40.

Miscarriage happens x percent of the time in women over forty, x percent of children have an autism spectrum disorder, older women are x percent more likely to have a child like you. They assign you an IQ of x. You count in x different languages. Sometimes x means no. Sometimes yes. You use toy engines to find the sum of x. Sometimes x equals why.

41.

A third of your tongue hung by a flap of skin, and I thought I would do you the favor of snipping it. Just a dream, but in my solar plexus I knew a careful fear as I worked along the seam, pink skin transparent, until the detached part sat in my palm. Then I couldn't find it, and your dental consonants were slurred by the tip missing against your teeth.

When I woke, I realized I had made a mistake. I tried to sleep back into a different narrative, one where I took you to a doctor who reattached the hanging, wet fruit of language.

Some dreams are not hard to interpret—that your words are ever tripped by an ungiving mouth or stuck in a loop in your head like a Rolodex spinning too fast to pull the card that says what you need to say.

Also, that I'm always at least half-convinced every decision I make for you must be the wrong one.

42.

They're slip-ons with three elastics across the tongue in dark blue, orange, and dark blue with a thin Velcro strap for snugness where our snagged hairs intermingle: mine, yours, your father's, the dogs'. The shoes are dark blue suede with lighter blue-and-gold stitching, just a little bit frayed. A lighter blue interior of mesh material is where your feet learned what shoes felt like while walking. The *Stride Rite* nearly worn from the insole and unreadable, it's still emblazoned across the top of the tongue and on the back flap at the heel, used to tug on the shoe. When you lift the flap, it's stamped ☆ MAJOR ☆ TROUBLE in a military font.

All caps remind us another day will never go by free of care. Each accident, trouble: broken leg casted for Christmas. Each incident, major: your father catching your shirt as you went over the ravine in Griffith Park. The shoes are a size-five, wide for your chubby feet, and the sole is unworn. You grew too fast. The rubber is flecked with white and treaded with concentric circles drawn through with slashes. The logo is worn from the heel, however, so that *Rite* remains. These shoes as passage then: the first pair you used to walk away.

43.

At your swim school, fountains burble, lilies bloom from planters, and the air smells of sunscreen. Phil Collins drifts from speakers dotting stone walls while parents with cameras sit under large umbrellas and instructors coax children across the pool.

I watch you leap off the white diving board, watch as you learn how to push off the wall and glide. Sometimes I watch you push off, gone below the surface before being pulled back up. When you are done, you pick out a red lollipop, which glows in the sun on the way back to our car.

Later, in Mexico with your father, me so far away, you fall into the pool only to come sputtering to the surface, back into the waning sunlight. From the deep water, you paddle to the edge, a boy, buoyant, better than expected.

44.

At the aquarium, we head to the garden eels peeking from their holes in the sand, and you want to stay because they seem to smile. You love the man in the diver's suit and the tank with the simulated waves, your face right up against the glass; then I look, and for a moment there's no trace of you.

The next day, I take you to the beach where black flies make undulant carpets of beached kelp. You have finally conquered the fear of salt in your mouth, so you let the waves knock you down with me tethered to you. Then you want to be knocked over without me, and I loosen my grasp, though not all the way, while the sea drags at your feet.

What makes some children wander into water? When I think *spectrum*, I think of light. When I think of light, I think of ripples. When I think of ripples, I think of the girl lured into a pond, the boy found in a reservoir.

45.

Today's paper reports that a woman rolled her ten-month-old's stroller onto a subway platform, then left on the northbound train. She must have struggled down those stairs from the street. I've asked strangers to take the foot-end as we hefted your weight down into the darkness, those arterial transit ways of the metropolis never meant for mothers with babies in prams. How she must have wanted to be done with her daughter's hungry mouth, those ever-grasping hands—no doubt dimpled at the knuckles, still full-cheeked in her infancy.

And just a news report ago, a father left his son in the oven of his car, the Atlanta sun baking, baking, baking. So we mourn, moving on to the next abandonment. And in other news, I bled again this month, the ticking slowed to a near stop, time dripping into the bucket of my own infertility. No more babies for me—this news personal, this news that breaks hearts, this news again about who has, has not, or God forbid, didn't want.

46.

At the Día de los Muertos festival, we pressed our way through faux Kahlos and faces painted with the harlequin of death to get to the bounce house so you could work off your weird energy. There must have been a hundred Fridas at the fair with enormous flowers woven through their hair. What a day—a shock—to learn I was with child again. I admit it is hard to see fortune meted out by blindfolded gods, hard to feel blindsided by uneven blessings. At the festival, it was harrowing to see revelers mock dying and all ascendant souls, though altars were placed on quiet corners where candles half-lit photos of full faces gone but not yet stripped of flesh. *Angelitos* are spirits of dead children sped into the lap of sleep, like my own good fortune spent later that week.

47.

Déjà vu was the same bright red gem of blood on the toilet paper the same profound cramping the same newsletter saying my fetus was the size of a poppy seed. So early such an ovum is just a whisper of maybe. One can barely call it a *miscarry* when what is carried is just a speck of desire embedded in blood. That night you curled in the dark of your bed as my face glowed by computer light. I haunted websites for grieving mothers and clicked on pictures of lost children to let mourning sicken me. To make me retch. To let it draw out every last clot. Those babies belong to others, but I have no faces for what I lost, so I co-opted eyes and smiles frozen in photo time. Eyes and smiles not mine.

48.

She turned slowly in my womb. In a dark theater, I felt her stretch, pressing down, as she pocked my skin when I saw her move. Then when I drove, she pulled toward the winter's weak sun against the windshield, rising to meet its warmth.

Pseudocyesis—

The ultrasound tech waved a wand and claimed she didn't exist, his screen a scene of empty, but every month I carried her dark hair curled wet against her head, her eyes closed against the red galaxy she spun in.

(Greek *pseudés,* false)

She cleaved to my ribs and hung like fruit on a vine, how my belly grew around her secret gift, girl eternally internal and always unknown.

(*kyçsis,* meaning pregnancy)

49.

At the human development exhibit, the eleven vats were all the same except for what they held: stages. I couldn't photograph the contents with the same camera I point at you, but here is what I remember: at first I didn't know they were real. Then, I read the plaques.

Their skin looked like lychee, small bodies curled as if still in utero, sex unfolded in miniature for all to see, and the largest, at thirty-five weeks, had a halo of blonde hair. And here is what I know: eleven times someone had to decide to put their loss on display in the name of science scrubbed clean of woe, their stories submerged in preserving solution.

50.

My ghost baby springs from a clot, a stolen heartbeat, and she settles into the arms of a stranger, but when I look again, she has the face of a stranger's baby.

My ghost baby slips into my womb and shifts but when I whisper, *Are you there?* I get no answer, only a trickle of blood.

My ghost baby wants me to take us to the park and push her swing until we are left to wear the town's frost and moonlight like a sateen sheath. She feeds endlessly, cries bitterly, and expects to be held and never put down.

My ghost baby lives in an attic where she pulls an old breast pump from a box and casts it aside, where she sleeps in your old swing until I am haunted by the ticking of its rocking and the sweet rot of its music box.

51.

A flip book of your years gone is history never to be lived again. Everything with you is first and last and never again. Your first shoes are my last first shoes. Your first steps are my last first steps. Aching pull of colostrum, pink of your infant gums, you fitting in my arms, all firsts of lasts.

We send your too-small things off to Goodwill—you at size three, gone. You in a high chair, gone. You in a car seat, gone. What is there to do but squint into a future that crystallizes like a glass city rising in the distance of a lonely highway? I'll keep driving towards a you I have not yet met because too much yearning makes a salt effigy of me, and I become the mother of all regrets.

52.

Tender is the afternoon in a Starbucks where muscle spasms conjured fetal movements. True, a friend sent talismans—onesie and beanie with ribbons like mayflies. True, the timing was uncanny. But at whose expense did those phantom kicks become the delusion I cradled in a theater while you watched Kylo Ren saber his father? How much for skipping wine at Christmas dinner? What's the damage for feeling the in-utero pull of yearning towards the warm, orange flicker of a fireplace? It couldn't have been real. Where were the darkening areolas, that rusty zipper, my *linea negra*, running the length of this skinflint purse? Where was the halted flow, that second-trimester glow? Still, I read about women who never knew until labor gripped them and a baby spilled out on the kitchen floor. If they could do it, then so could I. Couldn't I? What price must I pay for my own betrayal? What would it cost to admit I was a victim of magical thinking? The bill from the ultrasound tech, who found nothing but a cyst, a blood flower on my liver, and a wasteland of gray space? You can count every lump in my throat, tally every drop of blood wrung from the meanness of this body. I have already paid in full.

53.

The bland face of a fertility doctor smiles up at me from a business card in my desk drawer, and the cloying folder, pearlized pink with egg encircled by sperm in the shape of a heart, is to be discarded along with a bag of maternity clothes.

Dollars we don't have for a fifteen percent chance, just a few follicles ripening every month, your mother on the cusp of a change she doesn't want: the arithmetic of her body's undoing.

54.

You say, *I don't want to calm down, I want to calm up.* I say, *I need you to be patient,* and you say, *Being patient is not available.* You say, *I'm upset because my other nostril ran out of batteries.* I say, *You're cute and I love you,* and you say, *I'm cute and I love you, too.* You say, *When I grow up to be a flying pest, I'm going to guard your apples.* You say, *When I was a baby, I had cutie marks,* and I say, *And now you have beauty marks,* and you say, *I have beau-ta marks because I'm beau-ta-ful.* You say, *I coughed up my tummy.* You say, *Does this splinter make me look fat?* I ask, *What do you want for breakfast?,* and you say, *I want silver linings for breakfast.* I say, *I love you,* and then I ask, *Don't you want to say "I love you, too?"* and you say, *I'm loading mama—you have to wait.* You say, *Mama, I want to drink a case of you.*

55.

I feel bad for kids unfortunate enough to dodge diagnosis, how soft science has failed them. You go to school with so many just getting by. It's sad to see them staring at their parents' phones, all set for middle management. I see how satisfied they are with playing superhero, how their emotions drip, drip, drip into the rain barrel you filled before you were even five. One tells you your shoes are ugly, one rides a skateboard, one already says *fuck*. To think they will be average while you go supernova on us every day. Half our world runs on your power. To think we won such a generous sweepstakes. Or, as you call it, *Sweetstakes*. Our files burst with paperwork detailing our luck.

56.

Sunday evening. The days have gotten longer, but they still draw to a close. We're the only fools here where the wind has whipped our playground by the sea into a frenzy, where the wind throws fistfuls of sand in our face and the palms wring their hands. But we don't care.

This kingdom is ours. You ask to swing tandem with me, so we share one swing. We're casting a spell over the land. You ask me to pretend you are a baby, so I swing and soothe your cries. We make believe I am comforting you, and you comfort me.

57.

There is that tickle sometimes at the back of the throat, a kind of stabbing twinge you can't swallow, or there is that sharp itch on the sole, unscratchable under sock and shoe. In each, relief is out of reach.

I used to drink whiskey and wait for the ice to melt into the shape of a fetus, as if that would get me what I wanted. Used to sleep my way into subconscious betrayal, dreams handing me my swaddled sum, as if that would get me what I wanted.

Though I am better now, sometimes I can feel a kite string tied inside cut through me when what I want yanks it, nylon cord wrapped in the clenched fist of a newborn.

Yearning feels like this, a sickening pull from the navel toward what one wants.

58.

Your favorite song is "Water" and your girl is Sarah and you want her to hear it but she's home, so you use your fingers to make a heart, then break your two hands apart. I hold each hand in mine to make two hybrid wholes, to mend, to frankenstein our beaters better again, then I snip her picture from a class collage. You hold it up to the music, then fold your hand-heart around it like a secret valentine.

59.

What is it about a sick boy that renders him gorgeous? Not Munchausen's by proxy, but some trial by fire kindled in your hearth, high color of fever staining your face with roses, other skin struck white, the black of your lashes resting on your cheeks like sumi ink on rice paper.

Is it how I can gather all of your heat to me and feel the fight that boils there? Is it how illness begets stillness and stillness makes portraiture? Boy in a mother's embrace—your head burning against my shoulder, your body overflowing my lap.

60.

Is there something wrong with him? The ski instructor asked in a heavy German accent after your first lesson on a warm day in winter, the snow more like slush, her question more like a sucker punch. I stammered something about autism when I should have replied, *Not really, is there something wrong with you?*

How does anyone play by a set of rules as arbitrary-seeming as why some ski lifts were running and some were not? Those snowmakers spit out icy pellets unlike the filigreed crystals that drop from the sky as if God were trying to prove he exists.

I don't know what you did to give yourself away, but I do know that you held your father's hand, body centered in its own gravity, and slid down the hill, approximating what skiing looks like to anyone who was watching.

61.

All those years adrift in our spaceship with its weird silvery angles and odd pinging, but now this therapy office where we have landed feels a little like your home planet. How good it is to be surrounded by creatures who look just like jostling boys drawing math figures onto the air as if it were a plane of paper and their fingers were markers made of magic. When the front door to this lobby closes with a quiet click, you twitch your way in and grab a wand from your pocket. Well, not a wand, really, but a stick of lightning to trace constellations on the ceiling. Well, not a stick either, to be honest, but a mind that makes these things out of dendrites and synapses while the rest of us from the duller part of earth act like we're the clever ones.

62.

The mother of the adult autistic child who still lives with her is ready to offer me advice in the ladies' room where I am cornered against the whir of hand dryers. Another sends me messages with names of advocates and stories of her own son's violence. I deflect, thinking you are not like them, just as they must have denied mothers of boys with no words who must have denied mothers pushing sons in wheelchairs through the doors of the neurologist's office.

Then at the 4ᵗʰ of July carnival, you, a misfire sparking against the night, your energy all wrong—there is the mother of the *typical* boy who offers me a look to say *I'm sorry*, but I interpret it as something to be slapped off her face.

It takes a while to strip expectations away, to peel off the layers until we're holding our child's happiness in the palm of our hand, as pure as the simplest silicate mineral, and to then say it is enough.

63.

We were deep into the plush monotony of sunshine, and the moon's dopey grin was like a punchline in the middle of noon's tedious blue. The iridescent fig beetles would appear in a week to gorge on the overripe fruit. Our neighborhood running lady had grown predictably tan and predictably outpaced me every time I circled the reservoir. The grass grew brown and brittle, and in the afternoons I hid in the shade of a lemon tree while you ran through community sprinklers.

We punctuated the long, hot days with shave ice, and the sky blushed coral behind the hill of houses once the day sweated off its fever. We watched it cool from our chairs around the glass table in the backyard where you drank coconut water. Can't we just hunker down into predictability? Let's praise it and a simple rolling forward of our years.

64.

The windows of the photographer's loft looked out on a panoply of other windows above the shuffling of cars and women in smart heels. From the sound system I heard Bryan Ferry remind me that I am a slave to love. I told the photographer about you, how you seem more indelible, apt to be here for good, and I told the photographer about my failed attempts for more. She offered *we get what we get* and *we all have our crosses to bear.* Because I was reminded of it, I mentioned the preschool teacher who finished *we get what we get* with *we don't get upset,* and I pictured that green popsicle melting down your arm when you wanted red. The photographer spoke of teens as feral, so I asked: *Do you have any children?*

I had a son, she said, *but he passed away.*

A cross hung between two windows. My apology hung in the silence between us. Then the photographer's husband lit a pipe, and I watched its small curl of smoke hang over the coffee table before it ghosted into the air.

Notes

The epigraph on the dedication page is from *The Runaway Bunny*.

The epigraph opening the book is from Jane Hirshfield's poem, "History as the Painter Bonnard," from *The October Palace*, HarperCollins Publishers, 1994.

The italicized line in no. 10 is adapted from Frank O'Hara's poem, "On Rachmaninoff's Birthday."

The two children's books made reference to in no. 12 are *Swimmy* by Leo Lionni and *Harold and the Purple Crayon* by Crockett Johnson.

Nos. 13 and 16 both make reference to febrile seizures. Although the medical field doesn't make a connection between febrile seizures and epilepsy, my son did develop a seizure disorder after having two febrile seizures.

No. 20: an MRI is usually required after a seizure.

As in no. 23, a person will often have an EEG done if they have exhibited seizure activity. Gliosis is, basically, glial scar formation on the brain, generally as a result of some sort of nervous system injury.

No. 24: Sometimes seizures don't manifest as grand mal. Aside from febrile seizures, which were tonic-clonic, my son only seizes from the waist down. Thus, he experienced what are called focal seizures.

No. 27 is lifted directly from my son's diagnostic paperwork.

No. 48: Pseudocyesis is a diagnosis found in the DSM-V. Per the American Pregnancy Association: "A woman wants to get pregnant so badly that she mentally convinces herself that she is pregnant. There are many reasons why she is not getting pregnant including infertility or simply coming up to menopause."

93

The California Science Center in Los Angeles has an exhibit of eleven preserved embryos and fetuses, as referenced in no. 49.

The last sentence of no. 54 references Joni Mitchell's song "A Case of You."

No. 58: "Water" is a song by Ra Ra Riot.

The Author

Sonia Greenfield was born and raised in Peekskill, New York. She is the author of *American Parable*, which won the 2017 Autumn House Press/Coal Hill Review Prize and *Boy with a Halo at the Farmer's Market*, which won the 2014 Codhill Poetry Prize. Her work has appeared in a variety of anthologies, including in the 2018 and 2010 *Best American Poetry*. She lives with her husband, son, and two rescue dogs in Minneapolis where she teaches at Normandale College.

THE MARIE ALEXANDER POETRY SERIES

Founded in 1996 by Robert Alexander, the Marie Alexander Poetry Series is dedicated to promoting the appreciation, enjoyment, and understanding of American prose poetry. Currently an imprint of White Pine Press, the series publishes one to two books annually. These are typically single-author collections of short prose pieces, sometimes interwoven with lineated sections, and an occasional anthology demonstrating the historical or international context within which American poetry exists. It is our mission to publish the very best contemporary prose poetry and to carry the rich tradition of this hybrid form on into the 21st century.

Series Editor: Robert Alexander
Editor: Nickole Brown

Volume 24
Letdown
Sonia Greenfield

Volume 23
You Are No Longer in Trouble
Nicole Stellon O'Donnell

Volume 22
Spring Phantoms
Edited by Robert Alexander

Volume 21
Bright Advent
Robert Strong

Volume 20
Nothing to Declare: A Guide to the Flash Sequence
Edited by Robert Alexander, Eric Braun & Debra Marquart

Volume 19
To Some Women I Have Known
Re'Lynn Hansen

Volume 18
The Rusted City
Rochelle Hurt

Volume 17
Postage Due
Julie Marie Wade

Volume 16
Family Portrait: American Prose Poetry 1900–1950
Edited by Robert Alexander

Volume 15
All of Us
Elisabeth Frost

Volume 14
Angles of Approach
Holly Iglesias

Volume 13

Pretty
Kim Chinquee

Volume 12
Reaching Out to the World
Robert Bly

Volume 11
The House of Your Dream:
An International Collection of Prose Poetry
Edited by Robert Alexander and Dennis Maloney

Volume 10
Magdalena
Maureen Gibbon

Volume 9
The Angel of Duluth
Madelon Sprengnether

Volume 8
Light from an Eclipse
Nancy Lagomarsino

Volume 7
A Handbook for Writers
Vern Rutsala

Volume 6
The Blue Dress
Alison Townsend

Volume 5

Moments without Names: New & Selected Prose Poems
Morton Marcus

Volume 4
Whatever Shines
Kathleen McGookey

Volume 3
Northern Latitudes
Lawrence Millman

Volume 2
Your Sun, Manny
Marie Harris

Volume 1
Traffic
Jack Anderson